ATOMIC

WITHDRAWN

The World's Most DANGEROUS ANIMALS

PAUL MASON

Raintree

www.raintreepublishers.co.uk

Visit our website to find out more information about **Raintree** books.

To order:

 Phone 44 (0) 1865 888112

Send a fax to 44 (0) 1865 314091

Visit the Raintree bookshop at **www.raintreepublishers.co.uk** to browse our catalogue and order online.

First published in Great Britain by
Raintree, Halley Court, Jordan Hill,
Oxford OX2 8EJ, part of Harcourt
Education. Raintree is a registered
trademark of Harcourt Education Ltd.

© Harcourt Education Ltd 2007
First published in paperback in 2007.
The moral right of the proprietor has been asserted.

Editorial: Louise Galpine, Rosie Gordon, Dave Harris,
and Stig Vatland
Design: Victoria Bevan and Bigtop
Picture Research: Hannah Taylor and Sally Claxton
Production: Camilla Crask
Originated by Chroma Graphics Pte. Ltd
Printed and bound in China by WKT

10 digit ISBN 1 406 20343 2 (hardback)
13 digit IBSN 978 1 406 20343 1
11 10 09 08 07
10 9 8 7 6 5 4 3 2 1

10 digit ISBN 1 406 20364 5 (paperback)
13 digit IBSN 978 1 406 20364 6
12 11 10 09 08
10 9 8 7 6 5 4 3 2 1

British Library Cataloguing in Publication Data

Mason, Paul, 1967 –
The world's most dangerous animals. – (Atomic)
591.6'5
A full catalogue record for this book is available
from the British Library.

Acknowledgements

The publishers would like to thank the following for
permission to reproduce photographs: Alamy Images, pp.
29 (Danita Delimont), **14** (Nicholas Pitt), (Plainpicture
GmbH & Co. KG), **28** (Roger Eritja); ardea.com, pp. **12
& 13** (M. Watson), **8 & 9** (Reg Morrison), **17** (Adrian
Warren), **26 & 27** (Francois Gohier) **14 & 15** (Ron &
Valerie Taylor); Corbis, pp. **7** bot, **20 & 21** (Royalty Free);
Corbis, pp. **26** (Joe McDonald), **22 & 23** (Joel Sartore),
18 & 19 (Reuters); p. **16**, FLPA/ Minden Pictures, p. **16**
(Mark Moffett); naturepl.com, pp. **10 & 11** (Anup Shah);
Oxford Scientific Films, p. **11** bot; Steve Bloom; p. **6 & 7**.
Cover photograph reproduced with permission of Corbis/
Amos Nachoumand and Corbis/ Michael and Patricia
Fogden.

The publishers would like to thank Diana Bentley,
Nancy Harris, and Dee Reid for their assistance in the
preparation of this book.

Every effort has been made to contact copyright holders
of any material reproduced in this book. Any omissions
will be rectified in subsequent printings if notice is given
to the publishers.

Disclaimer

Contents

Some words are printed in bold, **like this**. You can find out what they mean in the glossary. You can also look in the box at the bottom of the page where the word first appears.

A KILLER WORLD!

Look at the map. It is your guide to some of the deadly animals that appear in this book. These are also the killer creatures you need to watch out for on your travels!

Golden poison frog

Location: *Colombia, South America*
This tiny frog is one of the most poisonous creatures on Earth.

pages 16 and 17

Killer bee

Location: *South and Central America, southern USA*
Angry killer bees can chase their victims over long distances.

pages 24 and 25

NORTH AMERICA

ATLANTIC OCEAN

PACIFIC OCEAN

SOUTH AMERICA

N
W E
S

Diamondback rattlesnake

Location: *North America*

"Rattlers" bite over 10,000 people every year.

pages 22 and 23

Bengal tiger

Location: *Central and Southern India, and Bangladesh*

Bengal tigers are famous for attacking humans.

pages 10 and 11

EUROPE

MEDITERRANEAN
SEA

ASIA

AFRICA

PACIFIC
OCEAN

INDIAN
OCEAN

AUSTRALIA

Great white shark

Location: *Pacific, Atlantic, and Indian Oceans; Mediterranean Sea*

The great white shark kills more humans than any other shark.

pages 6 and 7

Box jellyfish

Location: *northern coast of Australia*

Box jellyfish can easily kill a human.

pages 14 and 15

WHITE DEATH

"White Death" is a nickname for the great white shark. It is the deadliest shark in the ocean!

Why do great whites attack humans?

Great whites attack humans because they mistake them for **prey**. Great whites prefer to eat seals. But sharks have very bad eyesight. To them, seals and humans look alike!

Killer fact!

The people most likely to be attacked by great whites are surfers.

prey	animal that is caught and eaten by another animal

A great white makes a surprise attack on a seal pup.

Great white sharks find their prey by looking up to the surface of the water.

Number of deaths each year from shark attacks:
66

This croc has pounced on a chicken and dragged it into the water.

SILENT KILLER

Saltwater crocodiles are the most deadly kind of crocodile. Every year humans are killed by "salties".

Sneaky killers

Saltwater crocodiles are sneaky killers. They creep up on their **prey** underwater. At the last minute, they leap out and grab their victims. Then they drag their prey into the water.

"Salties" attack anything that invades their **territory**. They sometimes even attack people in boats.

Killer fact!

One night in World War II (1939–1945), saltwater crocodiles killed 980 Japanese soldiers.

territory   area of land that is used by an animal or group of animals

STALKING THE FOREST

Tigers used to kill hundreds of people each year in India. Even today, there are still man-eaters around!

Why do tigers attack?

Tigers normally eat deer or wild pigs. These animals can run very fast. If a tiger is sick or injured it may not be able to catch them. Then the tigers may attack people instead.

Tigers are dangerous. They are now also **endangered**. This is because humans have killed too many of them.

Killer fact!

In the 1930s, the "Champawat Tiger" killed 436 people in India!

endangered   in danger of dying out

Male tigers are huge. They can be 3 metres (10 feet) long!

These men wear masks on the backs of their heads. This fools the tigers and stops them attacking from behind!

The piranha's teeth can rip flesh from bones.

SMALL BUT TOUGH

Piranha fish live in rivers in South America (see map on page 4). They are small, but very fierce.

Feeding frenzy

When a group of piranhas attacks, it is called a **"feeding frenzy"**. A feeding frenzy can quickly take all the flesh from a body.

The number of piranhas has grown recently. New **dams** have created still, protected water. This means there are extra places for piranhas to have young. The piranhas attack when people go swimming!

Killer fact!

The strangest attack by a piranha happened at an airport. The fish leapt out of its container and bit someone!

dam	wall that is built across a river to create a lake of water
feeding frenzy	when a group of animals all attack at the same time

MYSTERIOUS KILLER

Box jellyfish are among the sea's most poisonous creatures. Their sting can easily kill a human.

Invisible killer

The box jellyfish is very hard to see in the water. Today, swimmers wear special suits to protect them from its stings.

The pain of a box jellyfish sting is terrible. Victims often die within two or three minutes.

This sign warns swimmers about jellyfish.

The deadly tentacles of the box jellyfish are very poisonous.

Killer fact!

Box jellyfish can swim faster than most humans!

This tiny frog contains enough poison to kill at least ten humans!

captivity   being kept within a small space

TINY BUT DEADLY

The golden poison frog is smaller than your thumb. Even so, it is one of the most poisonous creatures on Earth.

The mystery of the frog's poison

No one knows where the frog's poison comes from. The same frogs kept in **captivity** do not make any poison. The poison may come from insects the frogs eat in the wild. If so, these mystery insects could be the world's most deadly creatures!

Killer fact!

The poison is in the skin. Just touching this tiny frog can be dangerous!

This frog's deadly poison is used to poison a hunter's arrows.

WET-WEATHER POISONER

The Sydney funnel web spider lives in Australia (see map, page 5). Venom in a bite from this little terror can kill a human in fifteen minutes.

Home lovers

The spiders like to live near people's houses. Male spiders do not like rain. In a downpour, they sometimes crawl indoors. The grumpy spiders then bite any humans who disturb them. A bite from one of these spiders means you should go straight to hospital!

Killer fact!

Only male spiders carry the poison that kills humans.

The cure for a spider bite is anti-venom.

fangs

anti-venom	cure for the effects of a poisonous bite. Anti-venom usually has to be given to a victim soon after being bitten for it to work.
venom	poison in a bite or sting

The taipan has excellent senses of smell and eyesight.

fatal deadly, or able to cause death

THE FIERCEST SNAKE

The taipan of Australia is sometimes called the "fierce snake". A taipan's bite almost always kills.

Two types of taipan

The inland taipan can grow to 2.5 metres (8 feet) long. It can also move faster than humans can. But this is not even the most dangerous taipan!

Australia's coastal taipan is not as poisonous as the inland taipan. But it is very bad–tempered. This makes it the most dangerous taipan around!

Killer fact!

Unless you have anti-venom, 95 per cent of taipan bites are fatal.

DIAMOND-BACKED KILLER

Diamondback rattlesnakes defend their territory very fiercely. Anyone who comes near a rattlesnake is in danger. "Rattler" poison causes dizziness or sometimes even death.

Sleepy rattlers

Rattlesnakes are most dangerous in spring. This is when they come out of **hibernation** (a long sleep). Like a lot of people, diamondback rattlesnakes usually wake up hungry!

Diamondback rattlesnakes hunt using smell. They can also sense the body heat of their **prey**.

Killer fact!

Rattlesnakes don't always rattle to warn their victims of an attack.

Rattlesnakes can launch an attack in the blink of an eye.

hibernation   sleep-like state some animals go into during winter. They stay still and live off their body's stores of energy.

This man wears special clothing to protect himself from the bees.

AIRBORNE KILLERS

Killer bees are ten times more aggressive than ordinary bees! The bees attack if their hive is threatened.

Deadly smell!

When a bee stings, it makes a special smell. The smell causes all the other bees to attack. The angry bees sometimes chase their victim for nearly half a kilometre (quarter of a mile)!

Killer fact!

Don't hide from killer bees underwater. They will wait for you to surface and then attack!

| aggressive | very likely to attack, sometimes for no obvious reason |
| hive | place where a group of bees builds its nest |

THE GRIZZLY BEAR

Grizzlies prefer to avoid humans. Even so, people are still attacked every year.

Playing dead

Anyone attacked by a grizzly could try "playing dead". This means lying face down with your hands behind your head. Don't move, even if the bear claws you.

Bear Country

All Wildlife Is Dangerous
Do Not Approach Or Feed

The biggest grizzlies weigh 635 kilograms (1,400 pounds). That's about the same as the England football team.

Killer fact!

An attacking bear can move at 55 kph (35 mph). That is much too fast for a human to run away from.

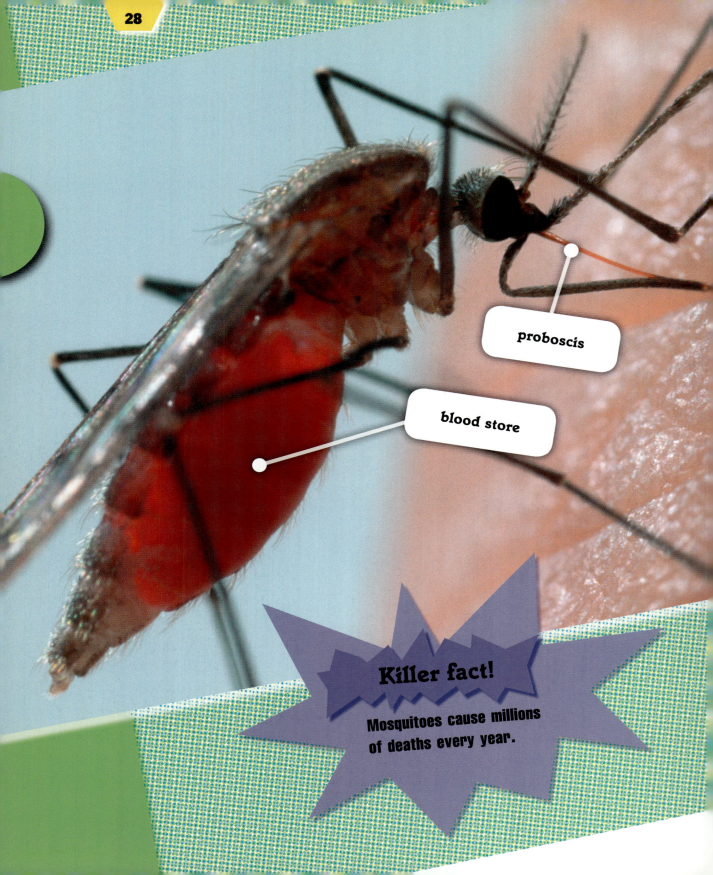

proboscis

blood store

Killer fact!

Mosquitoes cause millions of deaths every year.

THE DEADLIEST KILLER!

Of all the deadly animals out there, which is the deadliest?

A tasty drink of blood!

The mosquito is tiny, but very deadly. Once a mosquito has found a victim, it slices the person's skin open. Then it uses its **proboscis** to drink blood. A proboscis is a long nose, like an elephant's trunk. The mosquito can pass on a killer disease called **malaria**.

People use nets to keep mosquitoes away while they sleep.

malaria	serious disease that can kill
proboscis	long, tube-like mouth part

Glossary

aggressive very likely to attack, sometimes for no obvious reason

anti-venom cure for the effects of a poisonous bite. Anti-venom usually has to be given to a victim soon after they have been bitten.

captivity being kept within a small space

dam wall that is built across a river to create a lake of water

endangered in danger of dying out

fatal deadly, or able to cause death

feeding frenzy when a group of animals all attack at the same time

hibernation sleep-like state some animals go into during winter. They stay still and live off their body's stores of energy.

hive place where a group of bees builds its nest

malaria serious disease that can kill

prey animal that is caught and eaten by another animal

proboscis long, tube-like mouth part. An elephant's trunk is a proboscis, for example. Many insects have a proboscis too, though theirs are always smaller!

territory area of land that is used by an animal or group of animals

venom poison in a bite or sting

Want to know more?

Books

* Dangerous Creatures, Angela Wilkes (Kingfisher, 2003)

* Sharks and Other Dangerous Underwater Creatures, Daniel Gilpin (Chrysalis Books, 2005)

* Spiders and Other Dangerous Minibeasts, Daniel Gilpin (Chrysalis Books, 2005).

* True Stories: Man Eaters and Blood Suckers, Kirsty Murray (Allen and Unwin, 1998)

Websites

* www.amonline.net.au/
  Get facts about the dangerous creatures that live in and around Australia.

* www.thebigzoo.com/zoo/
  Find information about almost any animal you can think of.

* www.flmnh.ufl.edu/
  Click on "collections", then go to "fishes" to read about sharks.

If you liked this Atomic book, why don't you try these...?

Index

Notes for adults
Use the following questions to guide children towards identifying features of report text:

Can you find an example of a general opening classification on page 4?

Can you find examples of non-chronological language on page 6?

Can you give examples of present tense language on page 14?

Can you find an example of detailed description of an animal on page 21?